FREE JAZZ

Creative Originality, Controlled Surprise

ROBERT FLEMING

With K Kelly McElroy

**To Willard Jenkins, a peerless jazz promoter and critic
who got me my start as a writer about this
Black Classical Music.
Thank you, my brother and friend.**

Page left intentionally blank

Table of Contents

Page left intentionally blank

Introduction

Sometimes even a "Jazz Snob" can be hit with cerebral enlightenment. The general school of thought is as reflected by the BBC documentary: *1959 The Year that Changed Jazz*. Thus "Free Jazz" is deemed to have a finite definitive conception.

The aforementioned documentary delineates some of the most influential groundbreaking albums that were released that year. The albums included: *Kind of Blue* (Miles Davis), *Time Out* (Dave Brubeck), *Mingus Ah Um* (Charles Mingus), and *The Shape of Jazz to Come* (Ornette Coleman).

However groundbreaking these albums were – and they definitely were – they did not just *happen* to be, like some Big Bang occurrence in the jazz universe. All of these albums have an embryonic genesis from past works and conceptions. The same can be said of what is generally recognized as "advant garde" or "free jazz."

I must admit that I was not fully cognitive of this creative evolution. But after reading Robert Fleming's: *FREE JAZZ: Creative Originality, Controlled Surprise*, I came away with a much more broad and complete understanding of the actual maturation of what most of us recognize as "free jazz."

Fleming's written discourse is most likely the most concisely logical explanation of this evolutionary musical process that I have ever read. It is like reading a voluminous jazz encyclopedia that has been boiled down to its essential essence.

I say it is essential reading for novice and expert alike. I'm proud to be associated with its publication and joining the many jazz adherents who have and are, currently, feeding the wonderful tributary of jazz!

K Kelly McElroy
Cleveland, Ohio

Page left intentionally blank

FREE JAZZ: Creative Originality, Controlled Surprise

"Be yourself. Don't bother about what other people
say, because you are you. The thing is to be just yourself."

- Thelonious Monk (1964)

I.   The Purpose

This book is a necessary guide for any listener of the most original of American music, Jazz, especially the often demanding, challenging, but ultimately rewarding "free jazz."

With so many categories of music to choose from, listeners can be selective, cherry-picking any genre from hundreds of thousands of musical product. Even jazz consists of all types of preference or choices. We hope to make your selections of free jazz easier and more attractive, with the four categories offered here:

1. EXPERIMENTAL
2. CULTURAL
3. POLITICAL
4. SPIRITUAL

The quality of these musicians and their music has always been recognized by the excellence and vision of the established labels such as Prestige, Atlantic, Blue Note, Impulse, Fantasy, RCA Victor, Columbia, ECM, A&M, and Arista. Every jazz lover knows the pleasure of listening to their creations. However, a great deal of free jazz music can be found on any number of independent labels including ESP Disk, BYG Actuel, Candid, Delmark, Flying Dutchman, Steeple Chase, and Enja.

Choices, choices, choices. It's like either playing chess or checkers. As the dynamo trumpeter Lee Morgan used to say: "Either it's hip or it isn't."

II.   The Heart Of The Matter

Free jazz, also called "avant-garde jazz" or "the New Thing," reflected the philosophy and politics of the post-World War II times. Some musicologists say this form of music was born in the mid-to late 1950s when a group of musicians decided to break off of the confines of bebop and expand the boundaries of improvised music. They wanted to think outside the box, to become much more spontaneous and adventurous.

The explorers of this new music altered the traditional chord changes, tinkered with the customary time signatures, creating complex lines of melody and harmony. They refashioned the basics and deconstructed the fundamentals with surprising twists of notes, colors, tempo, and accents.

"Jazz is the big brother of Revolution," trumpeter Miles Davis said. "Revolution follows it around."

It was the turbulent time of the Cold War, the capitalism vs. communism, McCarthy with hunts, and the civil rights protests of Little Rock and Montgomery in late fifties. Although the music mavens tried to control the bebop market, the musicians revolted, turning the spirit of the music inward, becoming reflective, with capable sidemen expressing themselves with unpredictable and crisp lines, aggressive and angry melodies. This was an incredible period of experimentation and improvisation in free jazz.

The limits of mainstream jazz and bebop were shattered by the trio of pianist Cecil Taylor, saxophonist John Coltrane, and fellow horn man Ornette Coleman. Nothing was outside the realm of the imagination. Each of these musicians took different routes to their goal, transforming the elements of harmony, melody, rhythm, and structure. The performers of Free Jazz shunned any intention of entertainment or pleasing critics. They probed relentlessly their internal worlds, challenging their minds and bodies.

"If there's something you don't understand, you have to go humbly to it," Coltrane said to a reporter. "You don't go to school and sit down and say I know what you're getting ready to teach me. You sit there and you learn. You open your mind, you absorb. You're got to be quiet. I've got to grow through certain places of this to other understandings and more consciousness."

Whenever something new and original emerges, there are often naysayers and professional detractors who consider themselves gatekeepers. For example, when they heard Coltrane, Taylor, and Coleman, they immediately classified them as frauds, bogus, and charlatans. They enlisted popular musicians to denigrate the new musicians, such as Louis Armstrong, Count Basie - even Duke Ellington, who later saw the light with albums with Coltrane, Max Roach, and Mingus. A lot of the other jazzmen within the conventional, commercial world thought these men wanted to destroy their music.

Under the banner of free jazz, they played music never heard before. They played in ensembles constant improvising, letting the music challenge them, sometimes even soloing without rhythm support. The music needed a certain technical brilliance, a more personal self-expression, and a knowledge of the history of black culture and tradition.

Again, the pioneers of "The New Sound" resisted the urge of business to classify their music, much like the creators of bop did before them. They just wanted to play, to create. For example, when Taylor was stunned as he listened to the direction of Coltrane's music on the saxophonist's debut Prestige album, *Coltrane,* in 1957. A year later, the pianist was also impressed with his second one, *Standard Coltrane*, with the rhythm section of Miles Davis. That year, Taylor released an album, *Hard Driving Jazz*, with the surging Coltrane. This was one of the pivotal recordings in the early years of free jazz.

Quizzed by music journalists about the use of Coltrane, Taylor, like Miles Davis, knew what he had in the musician: "Coltrane's tone is beautiful because it's functional. In other words, it is always involved in saying something. You can't separate the means of the music that a man uses to say something. Technique is not separated from its content in a great artist."

Coltrane often blew his horn until his mouth bled. He kept pursuing the lines of sound, constantly pressing his physical limits, sometimes fueling that demand with drugs. He drove himself relentlessly, making the other members in his group better. That was what Taylor saw and heard.

"Improvisation is the ability to talk to oneself," Taylor, a percussive pianist like Duke and Monk, mused after witnessing Trane putting the sax fiercely through its paces.

On the other hand, Ornette Coleman, a Texan who grew up playing in several R&B bands, listened to Charlie Parker, and thought something was missing from bop and the old standards. When he moved to New Orleans, his music was not well received, so he went to the City of the Angels. In 1956, he formed his landmark band there with drummer Billy Higgins, bassist Charlie Haden and Don Cherry on pocket trumpet. A pickup band was used to record two fine albums on LA's Contemporary, *Something Else* (1958) and *Tomorrow Is The Question* (1959). Then the original group signed to Atlantic Records where the essential music was finished within a short time: *Change Of The Century* (1959), *The Shape Of Jazz To Come* (1959), *This Is Our Music (1961), Ornette (1961), Ornette N Tenor* (1961), and *Free Jazz* with Eric Dolphy on bass clarinet and trumpeter Freddie Hubbard.

"Jazz is the only music in which the same note can be played night after night but different each time," said Coleman, who sometimes played a plastic saxophone for its non-traditional sound. He often told reporters that he wanted his sound to be very similar to a human voice. But there was more to Coleman's unconventional approach - to his style.

Questioned about this "New Thing," saxophonist Ornette Coleman noted its ingredients: "The only thing that can change sound is emotion. Other stuff gets in the way and makes it sound like noise. But emotion actually changes sound, which means that emotion is ten times more pure than sound."

Rahsaan Roland Kirk, another horn man, called this "Black Classical Music," meaning this could no longer be termed whorehouse music or speakeasy entertainment. In other words, innovation embraced tradition. Throughout its heyday, the established critics attacked the music every chance they could, publishing long, harsh critiques against everything affiliated with free jazz.

If it could not find commercial success and nobody bought its albums, the music would self-destruct, the critics believed. They banked that the improvised music would never be showcased on radio or TV or the concert hall. Even the established jazz magazines had its distractors, giving lousy reviews to the performances of the musicians or no stars for quality recorded product. Everything wore a label or category for commercial value.

"When musicians get put into these categories, their expectations are limited," noted trumpeter Lester Bowie, of the Association for the Advancement of Creative Musicians and later the Art Ensemble of Chicago. "They say, 'Well okay, free jazz – bam!' That means this. Traditional jazz – that means that. So they can break it down easily. But music is not really like that."

As Ornette explained there were no boundaries to music, some of the free jazz pioneers used a foundation of black gospel music and the blues, putting their unique slant to the styles, turning their compositions inside out. The players wanted to inspire some emotions in the listeners, other than a finger-popping or toe-tapping feeling. They wanted the power of the music to hold the listener spell-bound, totally entranced.

Yes, these new sounds challenged the jazz listeners. The majority of the musicians acknowledged that this style was not suited to everyone; that it challenged the performers as well. But when it clicked in the hallowed atmosphere of a club and involved the audience, it made complete logical sense.

These cats were bold, outrageous, and took chances. The charts of the new music were daring and required superior chops. Some critics said it was racist and excluded white listeners and musicians. Like early rap and hip-hop, this free jazz was played by groups of black musicians content to perform before small crowds, not in concert halls. Often, it clicked in the hallowed atmosphere of a club and completely involved the audience.

There was more to Coleman's unconventional approach to his style. Rather than a cold, clinical sound and disciplined themes which showed off his talent, he wrote compositions that appealed to the ear and spirit, going often to unplanned discoveries in pitch, harmony, and melody. He also did away with the use of piano, freeing up the group to explore unaccented rhythms. An Ornette Coleman tune, as writer Amiri Baraka once said, could make you cry.

Like Coltrane, Coleman, ever the rebel, wanted to affect change inside himself as well as the outer world. "I decided, if I'm going to be poor and black and all, the least thing I'm going to do is to try and find out who I am," he noted. "I created everything about me."

At the beginning of the 1960s, a series of events rocked not only America but the world: JFK's Camelot, more American involvement in Vietnam, the Beatles, the CIA's Bay of Pigs invasion, the Cuban missile crisis, the Algerian war, and a number of revolts from former African colonial nations. Meanwhile, the trailblazers in free jazz adjusted their sights from their internal world to expand to pressing political and cultural issues affecting their community. In fact, some critics complained they were become too political and non-commercial.

Charles Mingus, one of the most accomplished bassists, composers, and bandleaders of this era, dismissed the label of free jazz and criticized the stress on profit. He knew about playing in noisy, smoky clubs where all that mattered to the owners was getting butts in the seats. The club owners were in a constant conflict with the musicians, and sometimes the customers too.

"Most customers, by the time musicians reach the second set, are to some extent inebriated," Mingus said. "They don't care what you play anyway."

Although the bassist was sometimes erratic and hostile on the bandstand and off stage, he was considered a brilliant musician, who understood the roles of politics and cultural to his art and community. When he saw the tragedy at Little Rock, Arkansas in 1957, where Governor Faubus sent National Guard troops to prevent a handful of black youngsters from enrolling at a school, he was angry at a federal government under President Eisenhower that allowed the police action.

The clever mind of Mingus penned a powerful satirical composition, entitled "Fables of Faubus," with a prayer totally mocking the non-violent civil rights movement:

"Oh Lord, don't let 'em shoot us!
Oh Lord, don't let 'em stab us!
Oh Lord, don't let 'em tar and feather us!
Oh Lord, no more swastikas!
Oh lord, no more Ku Klux Klan!

Two, four, six, eight
They brainwash and teach you hate."

Again, Mingus celebrated the breath of our culture and humanity with music recorded on the Candid and Atlantic labels. Some of his notable offerings are: *Pithecanthropus Erectus* (1956), *The Clown* (1957), *Tonight At Noon* (1959), *Blues & Roots* (1959), *Mingus Ah Um* (1959), *Mingus – Oh Yeah* (1961) and *Mingus Mingus Mingus* (1961).

"If someone has been escaping reality," the musician explained. "I don't expect him to dig my music."

That view was shared by the great drummer Max Roach, who blended a concoction of history, culture, and politics into his music. He understood his people needed more than a finger-snapping beat or a hip-swaying rhythm. They, he thought, needed to be reminded of the talents and achievements of their ancestors and their glorious past.

"The artist should reflect the tempo of his time," the drummer said. "He should also endeavor to bring changes where possible. The newspapers are filled with cries from every corner of the world. It is impossible for a man to escape the world. There are no ivory towers."

At the beginning of the 1960s, Roach recorded several essential albums, becoming a political activist as well: *We Insist! Freedom Now Suite* (1960), *Percussion Bitter Sweet* (1961), and *Speak Brother Speak* (1962). The jazz world was astonished by the variety and themes of these acclaimed releases.

While discussing the history of the music, we should deal with its cultural aspect. None of the icons here would label their sound as free jazz. But all of them cited their sound had influenced every genre, including the groove-soul-funk field, where the horns took on a much freer form or the rhythms from the drummers who imitated those of Max Roach, Tony Williams, Andrew Cyrille, or Sunny Murray. Through the late 1950s to the 1960s, even jazz purists had to admit that the consumers sometimes found the elements of free jazz mixed with funk and soul sounds. The faithful followers of the music considered it as a part of a musical and cultural continuum, one continuous process. Or as said by Julius Hemphill, a saxophonist with the World Saxophone Quartet; there was no difference between Sun Ra and Aretha Franklin.

Secular or sacred, it's all the same.

"We should know about our history, but we should not be so locked into our history that it keeps us from evolving new sounds," noted Archie

Shepp. "Everything counts. Still, you can't ignore Coltrane today or even Cecil Taylor."

But the entries in the culture section cannot be fit into a modernism category or any convenient cubbyhole. For the players of this unconventional music, performing in a variety of settings only sharpened their chops and expanded their awareness of the totality of the art.

"If I can play as many things as I can, or try to play as many things it makes me better to play many things in compositions, in tunes," Oliver Lake, another avant-garde reed player, added. "Playing many things in composition, in tunes that have changes, in tunes that just involve me creating from the audience or whatever."

The last section of the book is of the spiritual realm. Some of the musicians testified that they had a spiritual calling, that the music chose them.

On the whole, the spiritual world emerged in the late 1950s when Sun Ra appeared in a series of Chicago clubs with his intergalactic message. One writer described the colorfully garbed space traveler as "the peacock-strutting conflation of Ra-as-cosmic emissary and resurrected Christ."

Following the quasi-hit, "Message To Earthman," the astral bandleader told the media that the outer space beings were his brothers, who sent him to the planet, adding a prophet is often ignored in his own country among his own people.

He released a string of independent albums to his loyal following, including *Super Sonic Jazz* (1956), *Jazz In Silhouette* (1958), *Angels & Demons At Play* (1960), *Other Planes Of There (1964),* and *Monorails and Satellites* (1966).

"We were doing the things the Creator willed us to do, to awaken the people to turn to the Creator, to prepare people for the New Age, the Space

Age, an age where all things are possible by creating a new art form," Sun Ra said to anyone who would listen.

To close out this introduction, the most significant influence on the spiritual sphere of free jazz in the 1960s was John Coltrane. The saxophonist joined the band of Miles Davis in late 1955, the year of Charlie Parker's death. He lingered there for a time, but left to become Monk's sideman for several months, and then returned to the group of the famed trumpeter. Addicted to several vices, Coltrane said he had a spiritual awakening in 1957, which lasted up to his death in 1967, except for short lapses.

Cleveland-born saxophonist Albert Ayler was a peer with Coltrane, recording for his label, Impulse, and watched his evolution in the 1960s. "John was like a visitor to this planet," he explained. "He came in peace and he left in peace; but during his time here, he kept trying new levels of awareness, of peace, of spirituality. That's why I regard the music he played as spiritual music – John's way of getting closer and closer to the Creator."

Not discounting the talents of Yusef Lateef, Rashaan Roland Kirk, Archie Shepp, or Sonny Rollins, Ayler, with his unique wailing style, added: Trane was the father. Pharoah was the Son. I was the Holy Ghost."

His wife, Alice, a noteworthy pianist, commented on the origins of one of her husband's most recognizable compositions, "A Love Supreme." John, she said, mediated a week before he created the music. He appeared, excited, and told her that he had a whole new music. It was "the first time he had all the music in his head at once to record."

One of Coltrane's prime sidemen, tenor saxophonist Pharoah Sanders acknowledged the man and the musician. "He didn't say nothing," he said. "He would just did things. He never said nothing. He just would do it and that was it. You were on your own. You had to be very independent to be around John."

With some of his more spiritual recordings, some critics wrote Coltrane soloed too long, soloed too loud and with a great deal of noise. What they failed to realize that the horn man expressed the emotional and spiritual anguish of his community still oppressed by hate and prejudice. His albums reflected the troubling brew of that yearning and pride, including *Impressions* (1963), *A Love Supreme* (1964), *Crescent* (1964), *Ascension* (1965), *Transition* (1965), *Meditations* (1965), *Expressions* (1967), *Stellar Regions* (1967), and *Interstellar Space* (1967).

Upon Coltrane's death, free jazz sputtered for a moment but righted itself. Archie Shepp said although the Master had passed, the groundwork was set to rouse hearts with his music and heal old wounds.

In the end, McCoy Tyner, a sideman with Coltrane, summed it up: "When a faith is never tried, I don't think he'll ever learn anything. You have to have trial and tribulation, or what are you going to learn? In other words, jazz is not going to be a dinosaur and stay around in one form."

III. The Continuing Legacy

If anyone thought the traditions of free jazz vanished with the passing of Coltrane, they were mistaken, for the pioneers of this music spawned thousands of players around the country.

Some of the more notable performers were: Randy Weston, John Carter, Marion Brown, Andrew Hill, Bobby Bradford, Frank Lowe, Bill Dixon, Gary Bartz, Sunny Murray, Roscoe Mitchell, Amina Claudine Myers, Henry Threadgill, Billy Bang, Leroy Jenkins, Hamiett Bluiett, Arthur Blythe, Booker Ervin, Jaki Byard, Chico Freeman, George Adams, Don Pullen, Clifford Jordan, Rashied Ali, Woody Shaw, Larry Young, Stanley Cowell, Tony Williams, Wayne Shorter, Booker Little, Sam Rivers, David Murray, Oliver Lake, Julius Hemphill, Dewey Redman, Charles Sullivan, Anthony Braxton, Dave Burrell, Leo Smith,

Mal Waldron, Steve Turre, Sonny Simmons, Grachan Moncur III, William Parker, Matthew Shipp, and others.

One of the old lions, Wayne Shorter, concluded about the limits of free jazz and its future: "To hell with the rules, I'm going for the unknown."

Robert Fleming
New York City

IV. Categories

1. EXPERIMENTAL
2. CULTURAL
3. POLITICAL
4. SPIRITUAL

EXPERIMENTAL

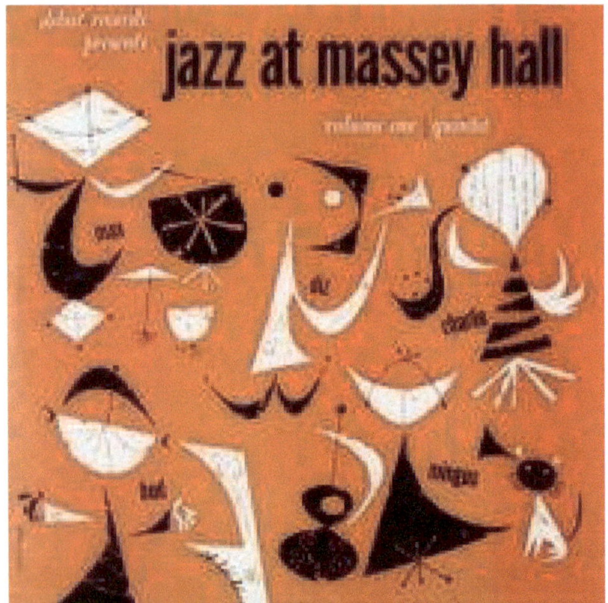

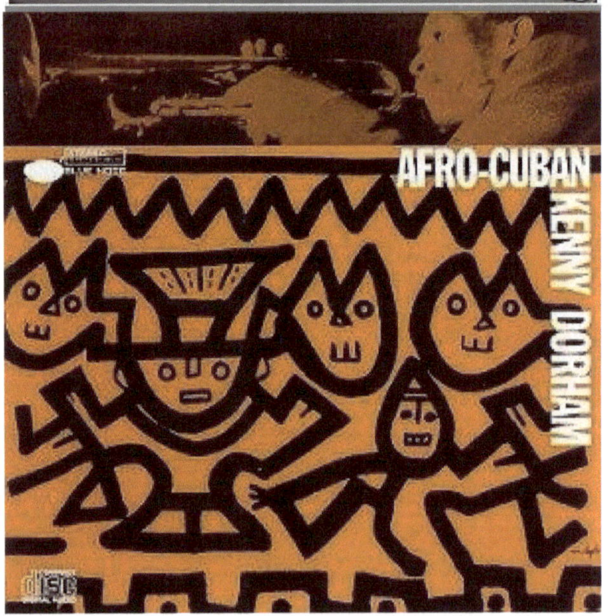

Jazz At Massey Hall
Charlie Parker
(1953)

Ray & Diz
Roy Eldridge & Dizzy Gillespie
(1954)

Afro-Cuban
Kenny Dorham
(1955)

The Jazz Messengers At The Café Bohemia Volume 1
(1955)

The Jazz Messengers At The Café Bohemia Volume 2
(1955)

Brilliant Corners
Thelonious Monk
(1956)

Jazz Advance
Cecil Taylor
(1956)

Tenor Madness
Sonny Rollins
(1956)

Pithecanthropus Erectus
Charles Mingus
(1956)

Saxophone Colossus
Sonny Rollins
(1956)

Super Sonic Jazz
Sun Ra
(1956)

The Clown
Charles Mingus
(1957)

Blue Train
John Coltrane
(1957)

Mulligan Meets Monk
Gerry Mulligan
& Thelonious Monk
(1957)

Sonny Side Up
Gillespie, Rollins
& Stitt
(1957)

Monk's Music
Thelonious Monk
(1957)

Way Out West
Sonny Rollins
(1957)

Sonny's Crib
Sonny Clark
(1957)

Hard Driving Jazz
Cecil Taylor
(1958)

Somethin' Else
Cannonball Adderley
(1958)

At The Pershing
Ahmad Jamal
(1958)

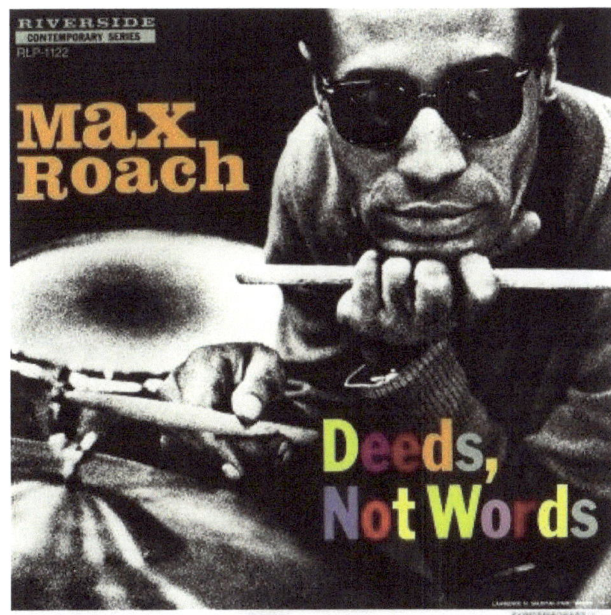

Deeds Not Words
Max Roach
(1958)

Looking Ahead
Cecil Taylor
(1958)

Jazz In Silhouette
Sun Ra
(1958)

Kenny Burrell & John Coltrane
(1958)

Standard Coltrane
John Coltrane
(1958)

Bean Bags
Milt Jackson &
Coleman Hawkins
(1959)

New York, N.Y.
George Russell
(1959)

Change Of The Century
Ornette Coleman
(1959)

Stitt Blows The Blues
Sonny Stitt
(1960)

Tomorrow Is The Question!
Ornette Coleman
(1959)

Quiet As It's Kept
Max Roach
(1959)

The Shape Of Jazz To Come
Ornette Coleman
(1959)

Screaming The Blues
Oliver Nelson
(1960)

Free Jazz
Ornette Coleman
(1960)

The Avant Garde
John Coltrane
& Don Cherry
(1960)

Out Of The Cool
Gil Evans
(1960)

The Blues And Abstract Truth
Oliver Nelson
(1961)

Into The Hot
Gil Evans
(1961)

The Outer View
George Russell
(1962)

Ezz-thetics
George Russell
(1964)

Out To Lunch
Eric Dolphy
(1964)

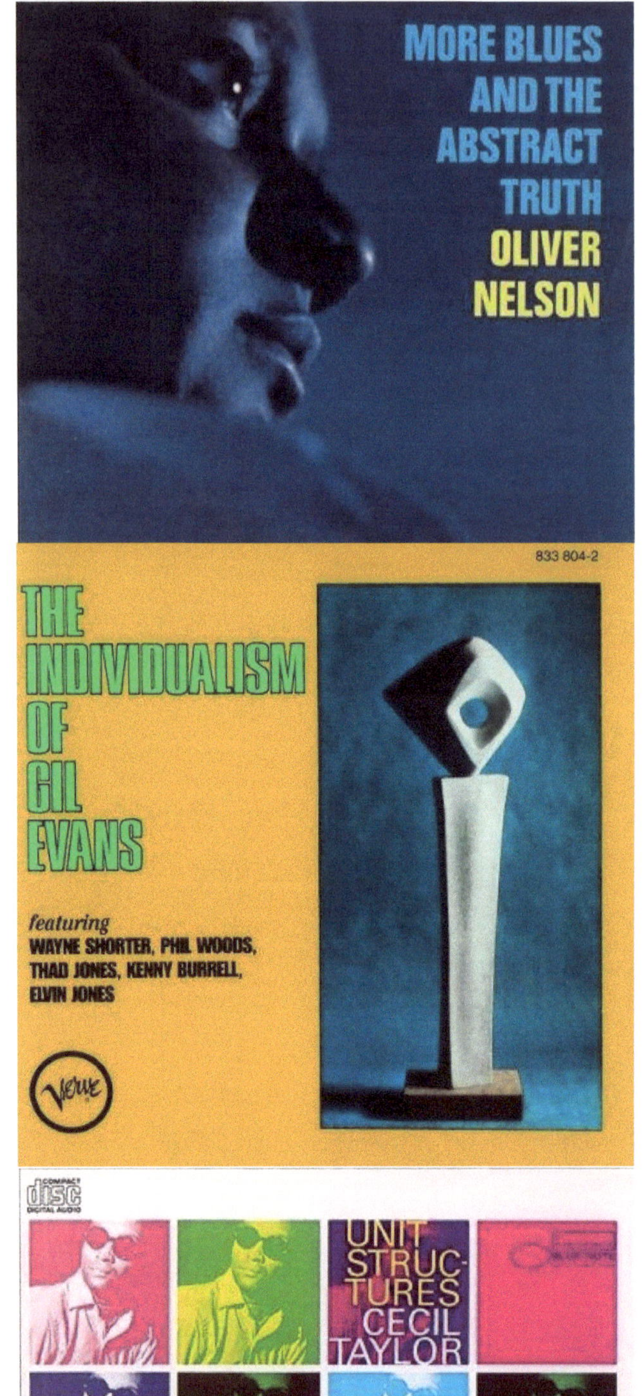

More Blues And Abstract Truth
Oliver Nelson
(1964)

The Individualism Of Gil Evans
Gil Evans
(1964)

Unit Structures
Cecil Taylor
(1966)

Where Is Brooklyn?
Don Cherry
(1966)

Sound Pieces
Oliver Nelson
(1966)

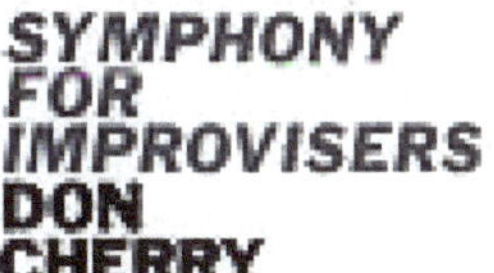

Symphony For Improvisers
Don Cherry
(1966)

Conquistador
Cecil Taylor
(1966)

The Gigolo
Lee Morgan
(1965)

The Procrastinator
Lee Morgan
(1967)

CULTURAL

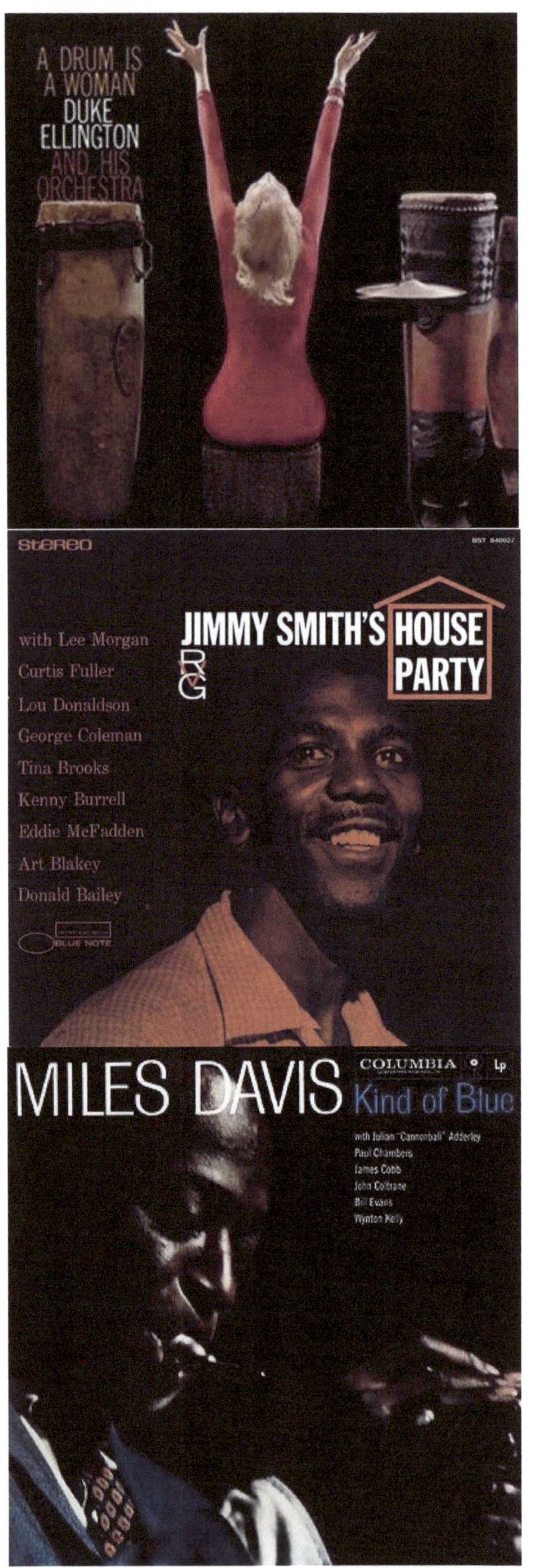

A Drum Is A Woman
Duke Ellington
(1956)

House Party
Jimmy Smith
(1957)

Kind of Blue
Miles Davis
(1959)

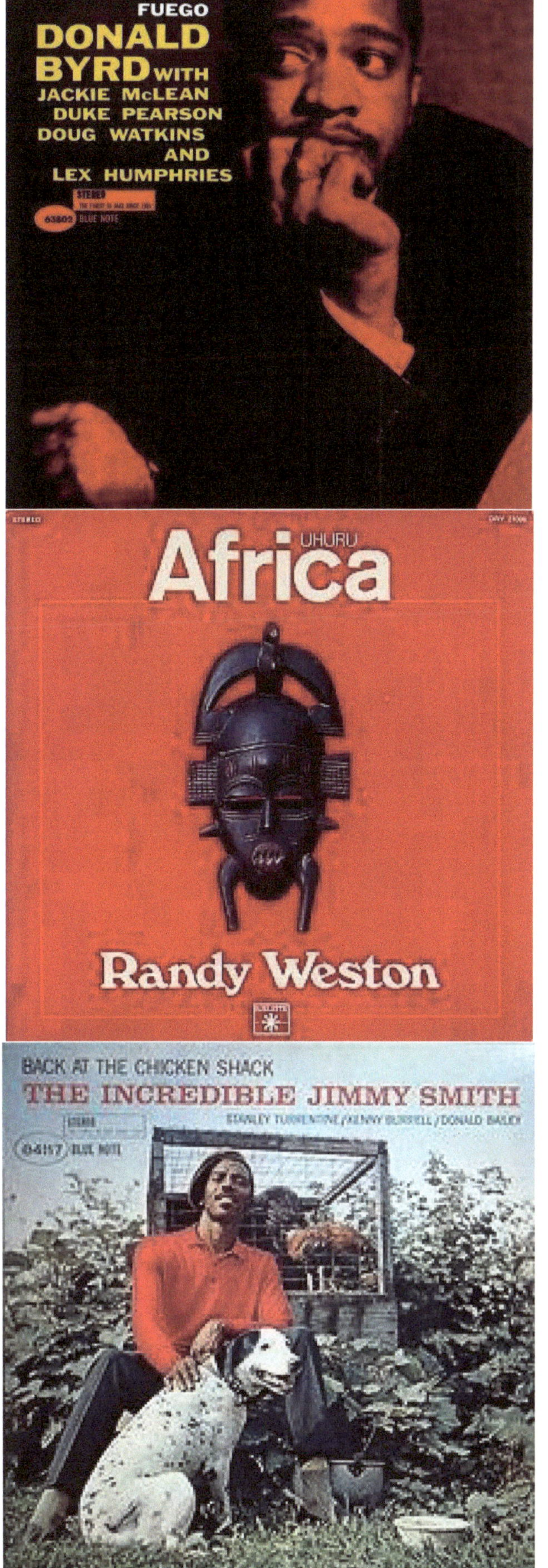

Fuego
Donald Byrd
(1959)

Uhuru Africa
Randy Weston
(1960)

Back At The
Chicken Shack
Jimmy Smith
(1960)

Byrd In Flight
Donald Byrd
(1960)

Home Cookin'
Jimmy Smith
(1960)

Midnight Special
Jimmy Smith
(1961)

Into Something
Yusef Lateef
(1961)

Straight Ahead
Oliver Nelson
(1961)

Free Form
Donald Byrd
(1961)

Eastern Sounds
Yusef Lateef
(1961)

The Blues and the Abstract Truth
Oliver Nelson
(1961)

Hubcap
Freddie Hubbard
(1961)

Money Jungle
Ellington, Roach,
& Mingus
(1962)

Out Of The
Afternoon
Roy Haynes
(1962)

The Natural
Soul
Lou Donaldson
(1962)

The Artistry of Freddie Hubbard
Freddie Hubbard
(1962)

My Point of View
Herbie Hancock
(1963)

Mo' Greens Please
Freddie Roach
(1963)

Duke Ellington Meets Coleman Hawkins
(1962)

Good Gracious!
Lou Donaldson
(1963)

Duke Ellington & John Coltrane
(1963)

Empyrean Isles
Herbie Hancock
(1964)

Evolution
Grachan Moncur III
(1963)

Some Other Stuff
Grachan Moncur II
(1964)

Matador
Grant Green
(1964)

Speak Like A Child
Herbie Hancock
(1968)

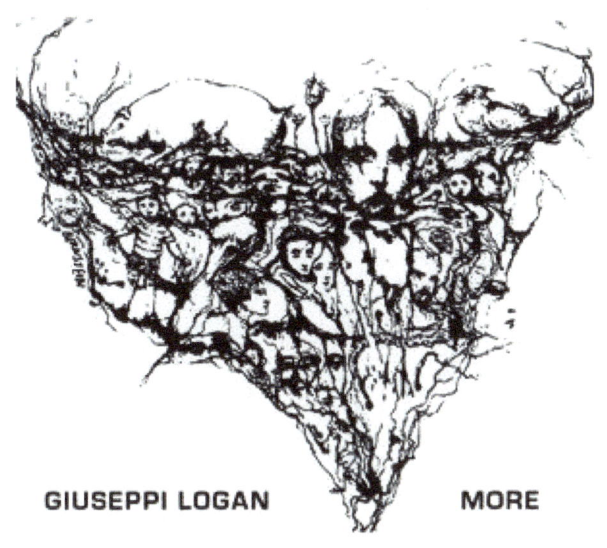

More
Giuseppi Logan
(1965)

ESP
Miles Davis
(1965)

Idle Moments
Grant Green
(1965)

Maiden Voyage
Herbie Hancock
(1956)

Brown Sugar
Freddie Roach
(1965)

Song For My Father
Horace Silver
(1965)

1984
Yusef Lateef
(1965)

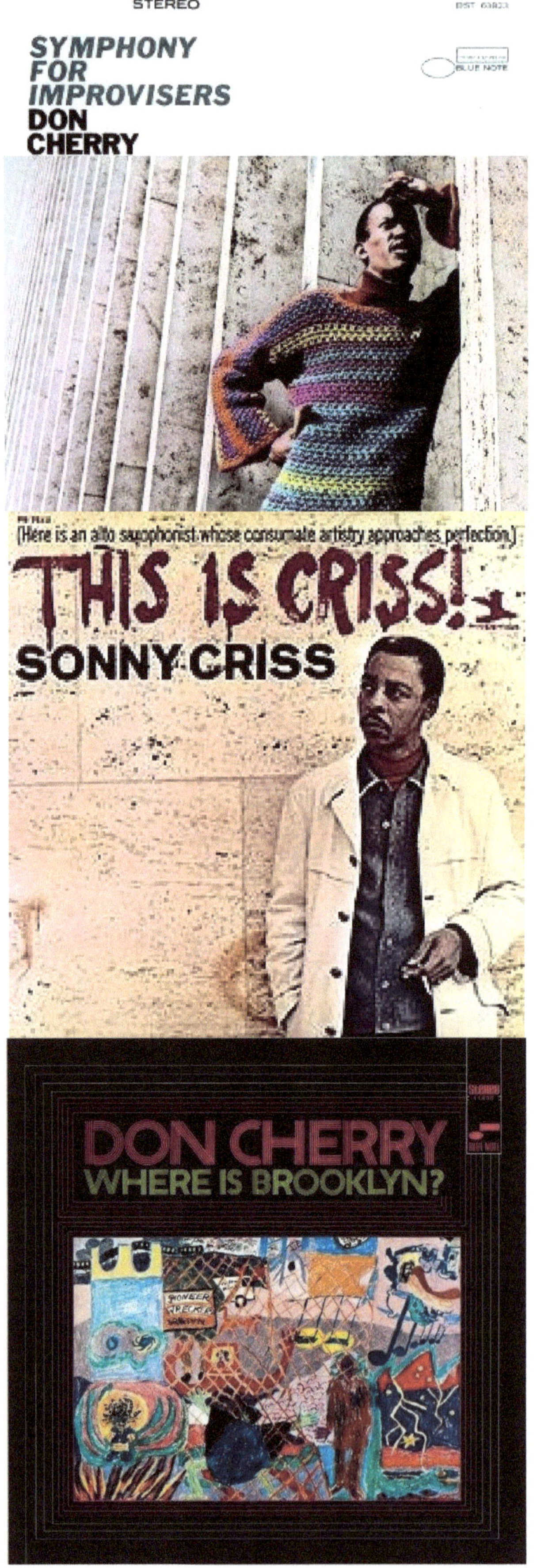

Symphony For Improvisers
Don Cherry
(1966)

This is Criss
Sonny Criss
(1966)

Where Is Brooklyn?
Don Cherry
(1966)

Mama Too Tight
Archie Shepp
(1966)

Sound Pieces
Oliver Nelson
(1966)

The Golden Flute
Yusef Lateef
(1966)

Far East Suite
Duke Ellington
(1967)

Slow Drag
Donald Byrd
(1967)

Tender Moments
McCoy Tyner
(1967)

Miles Smiles
Miles Davis
(1967)

Sonny's Dream
Sonny Criss
(1968)

Extensions
McCoy Tyner
(1970)

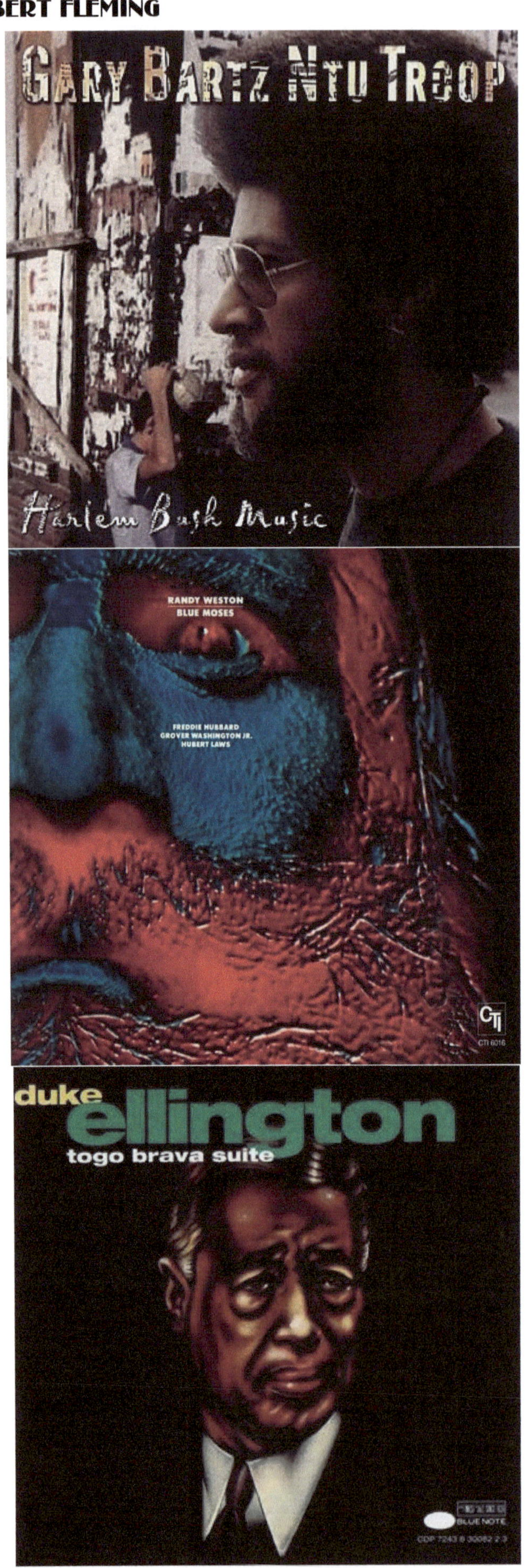

Harlem Bush
Music
Gary Bartz
(1971)

Blue Moses
Randy Weston
(1972)

Togo Brava
Suite
Duke Ellington
(1972)

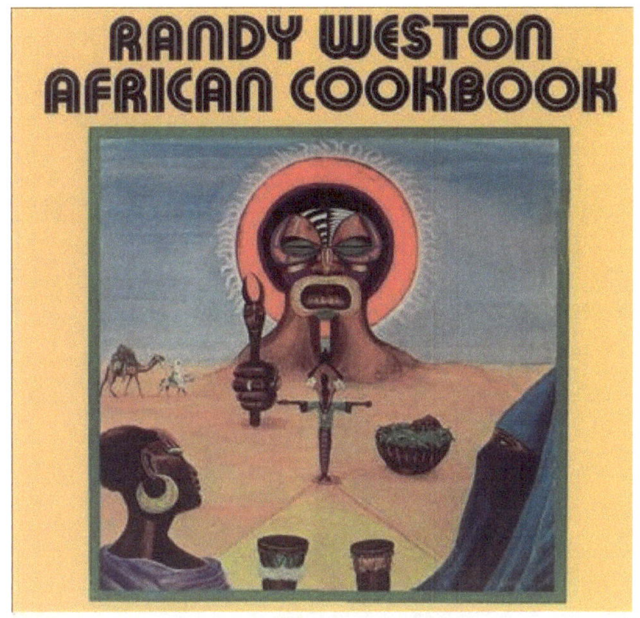

African Cookbook
Randy Weston
(1972)

Geechee
Recollections
Marion Brown
(1973)

Tanjah
Randy Weston
(1973)

Sweet Earth Flying
Marion Brown
(1974)

I've Known Rivers And Other Bodies
Gary Bartz
(1974)

Vista
Marion Brown
(1975)

Coon Bid'ness
Julius Hemphill
(1975)

Stolen Moments
Oliver Nelson
(1975)

Raw Materials
and
Residuals
Julius Hemphill
(1978)

**Fat Man And
The
Hard Blues**
Julius Hemphill
(1991)

Yonn-De
David Murray
(2002)

Gwotet
David Murray
(2004)

POLITICAL

The Rat Race Blues
Gigi Gryce
(1960)

We Insist! Freedom Now Suite
Max Roach
(1960)

Further Definitions
Benny Carter &
Orchestra
(1961)

The Freedom Rider
Art Blakey
(1961)

Let Freedom Ring
Jackie McLean
(1962)

Coltrane Live At Birdland
John Coltrane
(1963)

Destination Out
Jackie McLean
(1963)

Vertigo
Jackie McLean
(1963)

It's Time!
Jackie McLean
(1964)

Free For All
Art Blakey
(1964)

Action!
Jackie McLean
(1964)

Black Fire
Andrew Hill
(1964)

Search For The New Land
Lee Morgan
(1964)

Unity
Larry Young
(1965)

Right Now!
Jackie McLean
(1965)

Contours
Sam Rivers
(1965)

Bout Soul
Jackie McLean
(1967)

Sorcerer
Miles Davis
(1967)

Respect
Jimmy Smith
(1967)

**Volunteered
Slavery**
Rahsaan Roland Kirk
(1968)

Nefertiti
Miles Davis
(1968)

Inflated Tear
Rahsaan Roland Kirk
(1968)

Power To The People
Joe Henderson
(1969)

Liberation Music Orchestra
Charlie Haden
(1969)

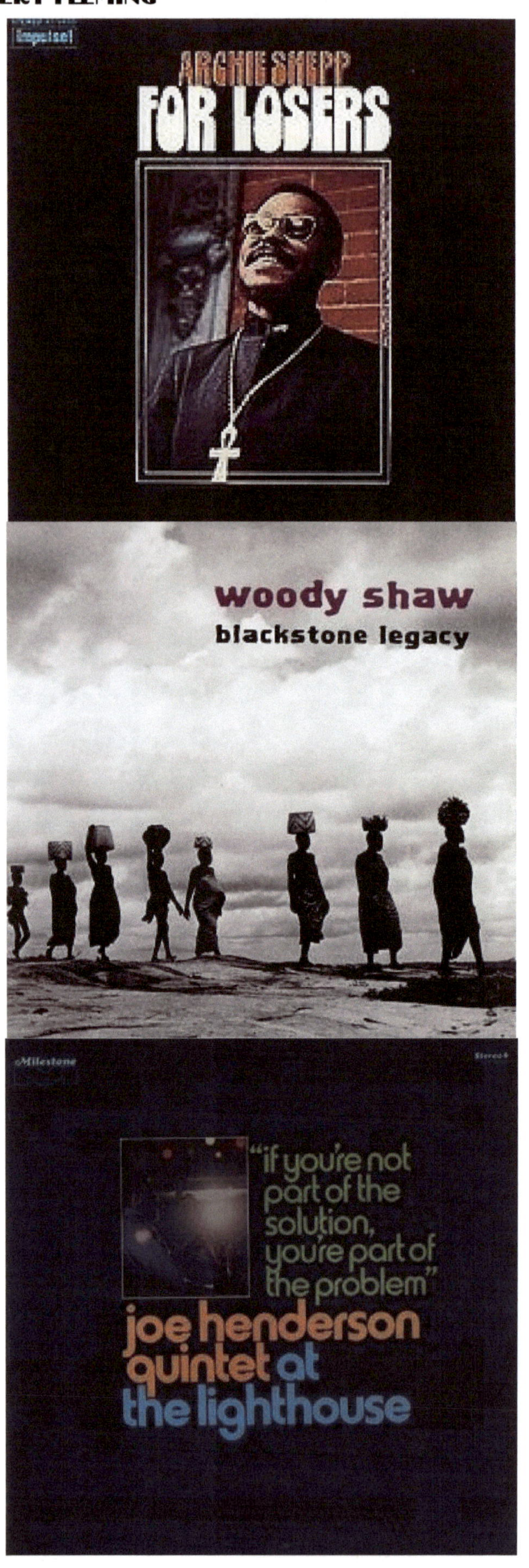

For Losers
Archie Shepp
(1970)

Blackstone Legacy
Woody Shaw
(1970)

If You're Not Part Of The Solution, You're Part Of The Problem
Joe Henderson
(1970)

Blackness
Rahsaan Roland Kirk
(1971)

In Pursuit Of Blackness
Joe Henderson
(1971)

Lift Every Voice And Sing
Max Roach
(1971)

A Tribute To
Jack Johnson
Miles Davis
(1971)

Attica Blues
Archie Shepp
(1972)

Black Unity
Pharoah Sanders
(1972)

Cry Of My People
Archie Shepp
(1973)

The Ear Of The Behearer
Dewey Redman
(1973)

Silent Tongues
Cecil Taylor
(1974)

Black Miracle
Joe Henderson
(1975)

Other Folk's Music
Rahsaan Roland Kirk
(1976)

Rosewood
Woody Shaw
(1978)

United
Woody Shaw
(1981)

The Struggle Continues
Dewey Redman
(1982)

Tutu
Miles Davis
(1986)

The Healers
David Murray
(1987)

Spirituals
David Murray
(1988)

SPIRITUAL

The Sermon
Hampton Hawes
(1958)

Black, Brown And Beige
Duke Ellington
(1958)

Giant Steps
John Coltrane
(1960)

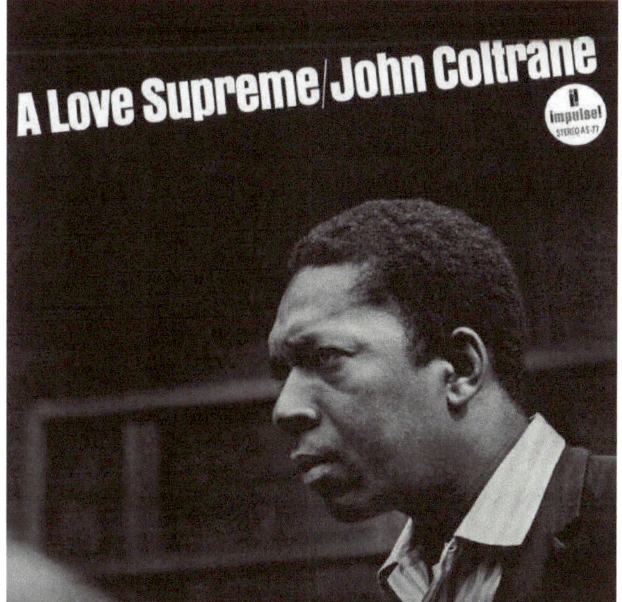

The Shout
Les McCann
(1960)

Impressions
John Coltrane
(1963)

A Love Supreme
John Coltrane
(1964)

Crescent
John Coltrane
(1964)

Into Somethin'
Larry Young
(1964)

Spiritual Unity
Albert Ayler
(1964)

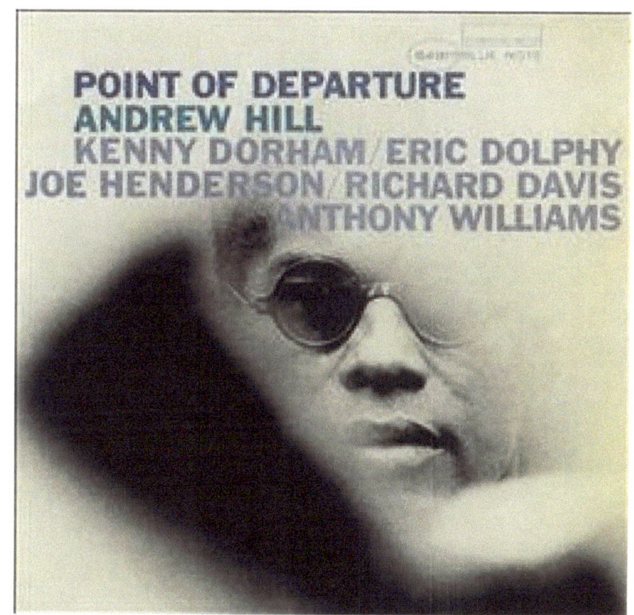

Point of Departure
Andrew Hill
(1964)

Compulsion
Andrew Hill
(1965)

Om
John Coltrane
(1965)

Transition
John Coltrane
(1965)

Selflessness
John Coltrane
(1965)

Meditations
John Coltrane
(1965)

Sun Ship
John Coltrane
(1965)

Ascension
John Coltrane
(1965)

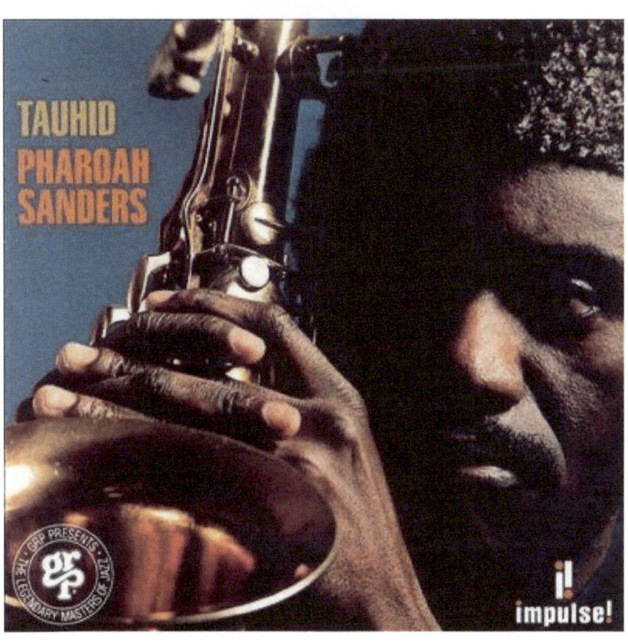

Tauhid
Pharoah Sanders
(1966)

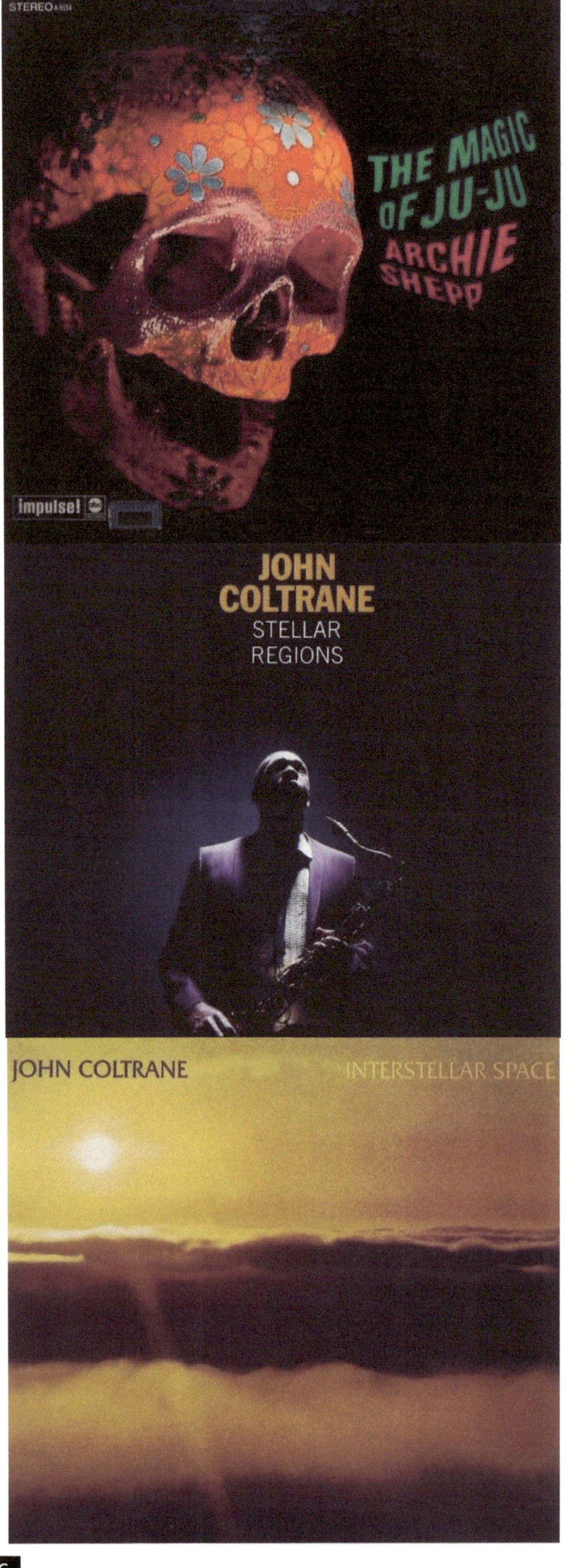

The Magic of Juju
Archie Shepp
(1967)

Stellar Regions
John Coltrane
(1967)

Interstellar Space
John Coltrane
(1967)

Love Cry
Albert Ayler
(1967)

Second Sacred Concert
Duke Ellington
(1968)

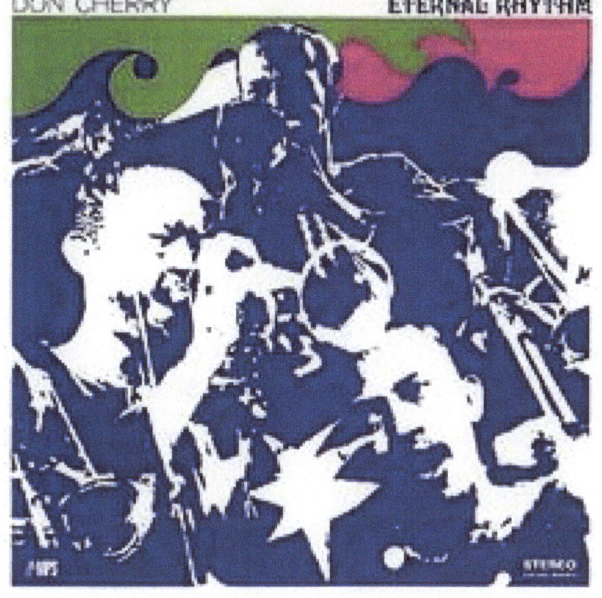

Eternal Rhythm
Don Cherry
(1968)

Cosmic Music
John Coltrane
(1968)

A Monastic Trio
Alice Coltrane
(1968)

Karma
Pharoah Sanders
(1969)

Huntington Ashram Monastery
Alice Coltrane
(1969)

Jewels Of Thoughts
Pharoah Sanders
(1969)

Music Is The Healing Force Of The Universe
Albert Ayler
(1969)

Journey To Satchidananda
Alice Coltrane
(1970)

Asante
McCoy Tyner
(1970)

The Awakening
Ahmad Jamal
(1970)

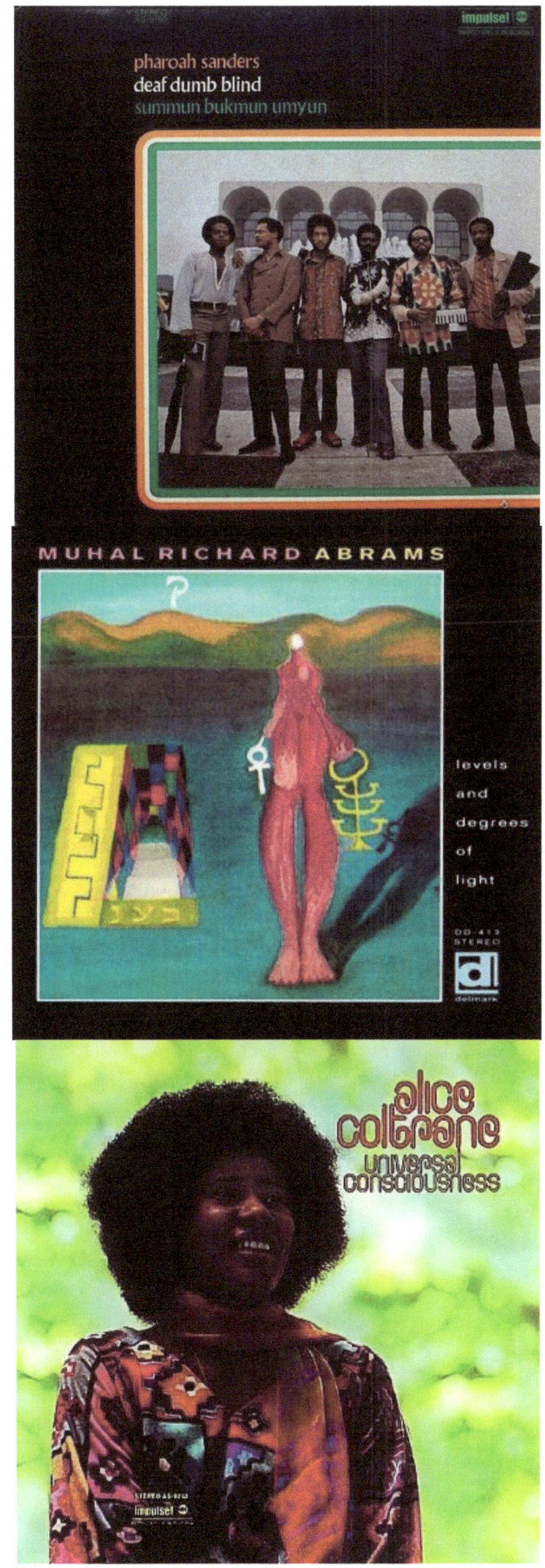

Deaf Dumb Blind
Pharoah Sanders
(1970)

Levels And Degrees of Light
Muhal Richard Abrams
(1971)

Universal Consciousness
Alice Coltrane
(1972)

Lord of Lords
Alice Coltrane
(1972)

Infinity
John Coltrane
(1972)

World Galaxy
Alice Coltrane
(1972)

Enlightenment
McCoy Tyner
(1973)

Kwanza
Archie Shepp
(1974)

Leaving This Planet
Charles Earland
(1974)

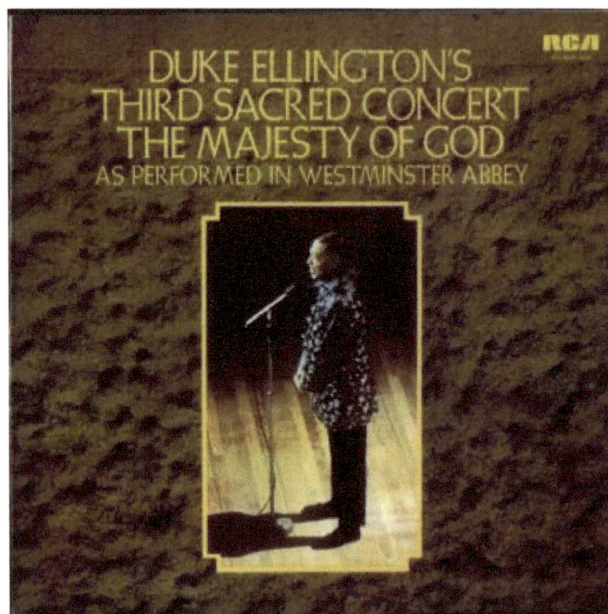

Third Sacred Concert
Duke Ellington
(1975)

Trident
McCoy Tyner
(1976)

Morning Prayer
Chico Freeman
(1978)

Journey To The One
Pharoah Sanders
(1980)

The Spirits Of Our Ancestors
Randy Weston
(1991)

The Highest Mountain
Clifford Jordan
(1994)

Divine Revelation
Andrew Hill
(1994)

Vision Toward Essence
Muhal
Richard Abrams
(1998)

Eternity
Alice Coltrane
(2002)

The Spiritual Side of Wynton Marsalis

Wynton Marsalis
(2013)

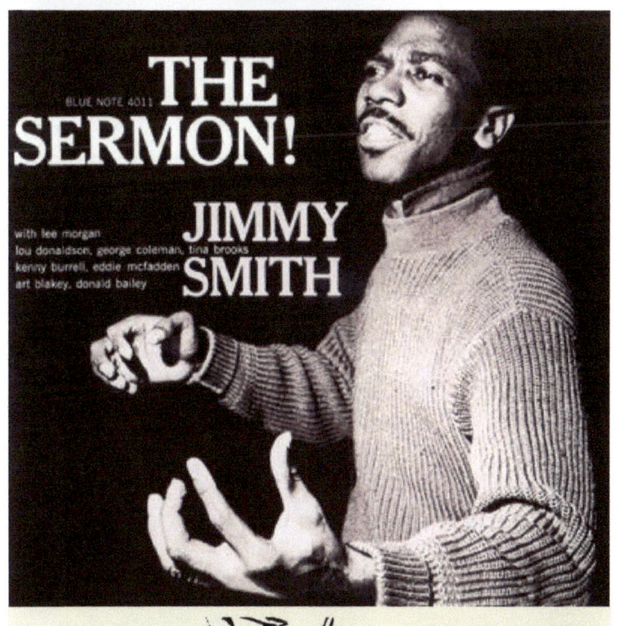

The Sermon!

Jimmy Smith
(1959)

The Congregation

Johnny Griffin
(1957)

The Quest
Mal Waldron
(1961)

Blue Spirits
Freddie Hubbard
(1965)

Feelin' The Spirit
Grant Green
(1963)

Members Don't Get Weary
Max Roach
(1968)

Sunday Morning
Grant Green
(1961)

New And Old Gospel
Jackie McLean
(1967)

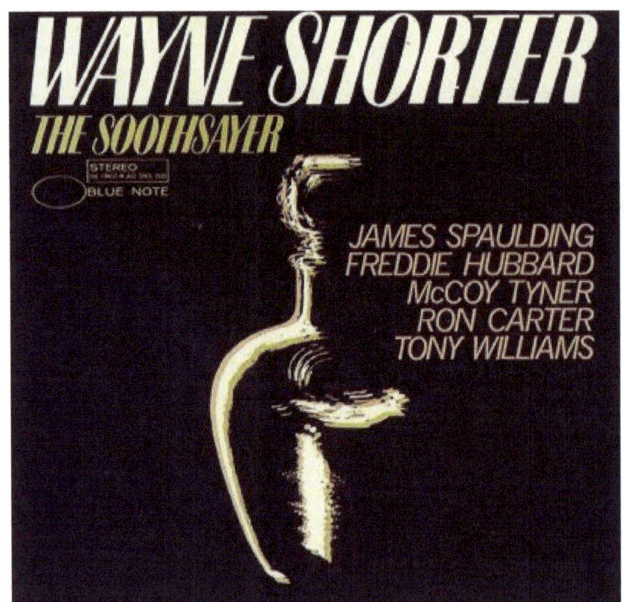

The Soothsayer
Wayne Shorter
(1965)

The Elements
Joe Henderson
(1973)

Song Of The New World
McCoy Tyner
(1973)

The Seeker

Azar Lawrence
(2014)

About the Authors

Robert Fleming, a freelance journalist and editor, formerly worked as a writer-consultant with ex-CBS News president Fred Friendly, boss of the legendary Edward R. Morrow for the PBS TV show, Media and Society, after graduating from Columbia University's Journalism school. Employed throughout the 1980s and into the 1990s, he served as a reporter for the *New York Daily News*, earning several honors including a New York Press Club award and a Revson Fellowship in 1990. He worked as a freelance editor and book doctor at Random House's imprint, One World. He taught courses in film and journalism at Manhattan's prestigious The New School. His articles and reviews have appeared in many publications such as *The New York Times, The Washington Post, U.S. News and World Report, Essence, Black Enterprise, Omni, Black Issues Book Review, Quarterly Black Review, and Publishers Weekly.* He has written several non-fiction books such as *Rescuing A Neighborhood, The Success of Caroline Jones Inc., The Wisdom of the Elders, and The African-American Writer's Handbook.* His fiction consists of such works as *Fever In The Blood, Havoc After Dark: Tales of Terror, Gift of Faith, Gift of Truth, and Gift of Revelation.* He edited three anthologies, *After Hours, Intimacy, and the Muntu Poets Anthology Volume 2 – 47 Years Later with Russell Atkins.*

K Kelly is an avid Modern Jazz enthusiast. He proudly owns a vintage collection of over 1000 classic jazz CDs. He authored the book: *Best of the Best Modern Jazz*, which is an effort to compile his significant knowledge of the genre to assist others who want to develop and enjoy their own modern jazz collection.

At the helm of Uptown Media Joint Ventures Publishing, K Kelly is following his passion of helping authors get their viable stories published. This passion has expanded to facilitate recording artists being heard, as well, via a label he started under the name Uptown MJV Records.

Best of the Best
Modern Jazz Recordings
Mid 1950s to 1970s and Beyond
The Definitive Guide to Building your Ultimate Modern Jazz CD Collection
K Kelly McElroy

FREE JAZZ

Creative Originality, Controlled Surprise

ROBERT FLEMING

With K Kelly McElroy